The Library of the Nine Planets™

PLUTO

Chris Hayhurst

The Rosen Publishing Group, Inc., New York

Published in 2005 by The Rosen Publishing Group, Inc.
29 East 21st Street, New York, NY 10010

Library of Congress Cataloging-in-Publication Data

Hayhurst, Chris.
Pluto/by Chris Hayhurst.
    p. cm.—(The library of the nine planets) Includes bibliographical
    references and index.
ISBN 1-4042-0172-6 (lib. bdg.)
1. Pluto (Planet)—Juvenile literature. [1. Pluto (Planet)]
I. Title. II. Series.
QB701.H39 2004
523.48'2—dc22

                                                    2003023219

Manufactured in the United States of America

On the cover: Background: An artist's rendition of Pluto. Inset: An
image of Pluto taken by Hubble.

Contents

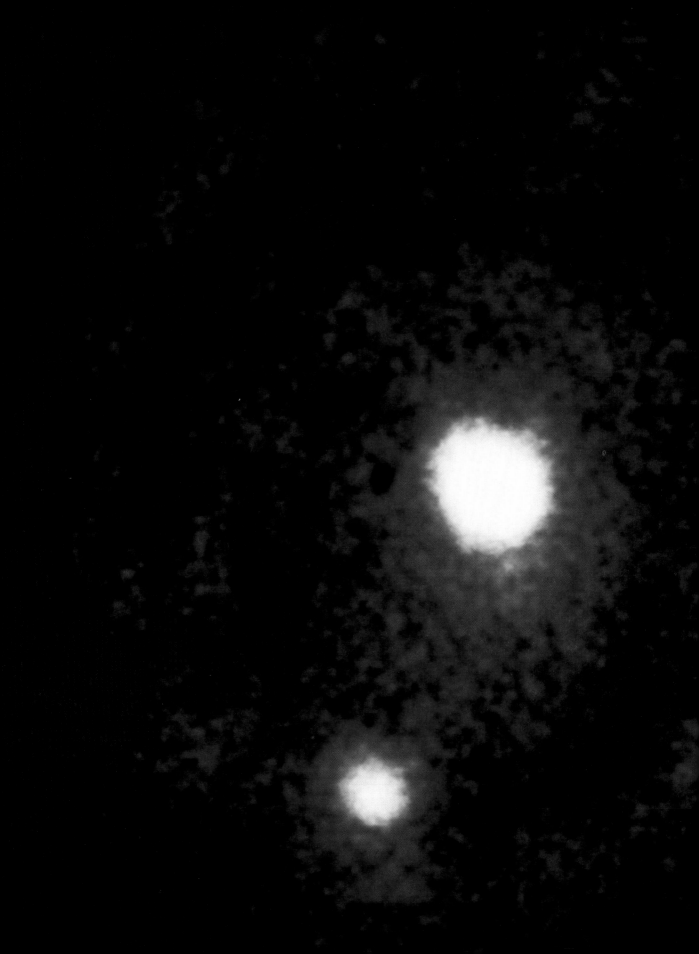

INTRODUCTION

Imagine you're an astronaut. You're hurtling through space at thousands of miles per hour aboard an extremely cramped and cluttered craft the size of a large jet airplane. With you are hundreds of high-tech devices—everything from computers to robots to special space suits and space vehicles—specifically designed to help you study your destination: the planet Pluto.

You've been in space for a very long time. In fact, you and your colleagues left Earth more than two years ago. It's a long journey, this voyage to Pluto, millions of miles from Earth. No one has ever traveled this deep into the solar system. You're charting new ground. You could say your mission is destined to make history.

It's really hard to see Pluto from Earth, but if you have a telescope you might be able to find it in your sights. But don't expect to see much. The planet will look just like a small star, little more than a tiny pinprick of light.

Pluto is very small even close up, at least when compared to Earth. If Earth were hollow you could squeeze more than 150 Plutos inside it. So as your spacecraft approaches this distant planet, there's not much to see at first, just a small speck on the horizon. But as you get closer, as surface features begin to come into view, Pluto's true character emerges. This planet you're about to visit may be tiny, but what better way to spend a day than by exploring it?

Before you begin, however, here are a few facts about Pluto. Pluto is the ninth planet in the solar system, behind Mercury, Venus, Earth, Mars, Jupiter, Saturn, Uranus, and Neptune. Pluto is so far away that light from the Sun, which supplies light to all the planets, takes nearly six hours to reach it—it takes nine minutes for light from the Sun to reach Earth. And by the time the light does get there, it's really dim: Sunlight is almost 2,000 times dimmer on Pluto than it is on Earth.

Though Pluto is currently considered the last planet in our solar system, it may not be for long. Even today, scientists are finding new objects orbiting the Sun, such as the planetoids Quaoar and Sedna, which were first seen in 2003. These discoveries suggest that we might soon find out that Pluto has another neighbor.

One

A Lucky Discovery

Scientists know comparatively little about Pluto—certainly not as much as they know about Mars or Venus. And it's not surprising why. Pluto is so far away from Earth you can barely even see it with a telescope, and it's way too far to see with the naked eye. Pluto is just 1,440 miles (2,317 kilometers) in diameter (the distance from end to end through the center of the planet). This is about the same distance as a drive halfway across the United States.

Astronomers, the scientists who study space and the planets, asteroids, comets, and other objects found there, have studied Pluto for fewer years than they've studied any of the other eight planets. And that's not because they don't want to learn about Pluto. It's because Pluto was the very last planet to be discovered. Before 1930, we didn't even know that Pluto existed.

Pluto's Discovery

Most astronomers doubted the existence of a ninth planet before the early 1900s (most believed Neptune, which had been discovered in 1846, was the eighth and last planet in our solar system), but a few forward-thinking scientists thought otherwise.

One of these scientists was a man by the name of Percival Lowell. In the early 1900s, Lowell, a well-respected astronomer from Arizona, wrote about what he believed was

Lowell Observatory, shown here, was founded by and named after American astronomer Percival Lowell in 1894. The observatory is at Anderson Mesa near Flagstaff, Arizona. Beneath its retractable dome is a 42-inch (1.07 m) telescope. The observatory now operates eight telescopes in the Flagstaff area and one in Australia.

another planet that was located somewhere beyond Neptune. He called it Planet X. Planet X must exist, he said, because the orbits of Neptune and Uranus didn't make mathematical sense. Calculations based on gravitational forces of known objects in space suggested that their orbits would fit one pattern. But real-life observations of these orbits showed that they were slightly different than expected. In other words, the gravity of some unseen object in space must have been pulling on the planets and changing their orbits.

William Henry Pickering, shown here, expanded on Lowell's theories about the soon-to-be-discovered Pluto. Pickering calculated that Pluto, which he temporarily named Planet O, must exist. However, Pickering calculated that the planet was at a different point than did Lowell.

Lowell began his quest for the missing planet by figuring its gravity into his calculations. For years he and his colleagues searched, using the highest-powered telescopes of the day to scan the night skies. They looked and looked, but they found nothing.

Lowell wasn't alone in his hunt, as a few other astronomers had similar ideas. One of these astronomers, a man named William Henry Pickering, of the Harvard College Observatory in Massachusetts, called the missing planet Planet O. In 1908, he published a report justifying his beliefs about this yet-to-be-discovered celestial body. Pickering's calculations put Planet O at a different point in the solar system than did Lowell's calculations for Planet X. Interestingly, Pickering also predicted the existence of several other planets in addition to Planet O. He called these Planets P, Q, R, and S.

For years the hunt continued, but it tapered off as astronomers devoted their time to other space-related studies. Then, in 1927, researchers at the Lowell Observatory in Arizona, which Lowell founded, decided to renew the search. Using their new telescope, one that was state-of-the-art and designed to peer into the deepest reaches of the solar system, they once again began scanning the skies.

A man named Clyde Tombaugh led the way, using Lowell's calculations as his guide. Tombaugh used the telescope to take photographs of the region of space where Planet X was believed to be, then he analyzed the photographs in the lab.

Pluto's Dual Citizenship

In Roman mythology, Pluto (also known as Hades or Dis) is the god of the underworld, a place where the dead reside for eternity. This is an interesting piece of information because, according to astronomers who have studied the planet closely, Pluto resides on the edge of two distinct space worlds. The first world includes the eight other planets between Pluto and the Sun, what we normally consider to be our solar system. The second world is not as well known and is called the Kuiper Belt.

The Kuiper Belt, which technically begins outside the orbit of Neptune (the eighth planet from the Sun), is a region full of icy objects that look a lot like comets. Scientists believe the belt marks the end of the solar system. They also consider Pluto to be the largest of all the Kuiper Belt objects. A few scientists even doubt whether Pluto is a planet at all and instead consider it to be just another large object in the Kuiper Belt.

Shown here is an artist's rendition of Pluto and Charon (*right*) as seen from space among other objects in the Kuiper Belt. Artists' renditions such as these are necessary because Pluto is too far away to photograph with any detail. Even the Hubble telescope, the most powerful telescope ever, takes photographs of Pluto that are not as detailed as we would like, as can be seen in the photo on page 18.

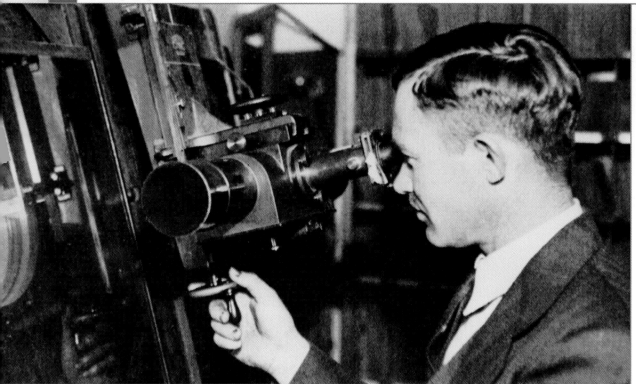

Clyde Tombaugh, shown here, is using the device that helped him to discover Pluto. Called the Blink Comparator, the device compared two photographs taken of the sky. By comparing the two, it was easy to see if any object changed position. After 7,000 hours, Tombaugh found Pluto orbiting just past Neptune.

Finally, on February 18, 1930, Tombaugh found what he was looking for. One of the many photographs taken with the telescope showed a faint object that had never been charted on any map. Tombaugh and the other researchers looked closely at the image, unsure of what to think. Could it be Planet X?

Tombaugh and his colleagues withheld announcing their discovery for almost a month while they worked to ensure that the object in the photograph was the missing planet. Then, on March 13, 1930, they came forth with the news. Planet X had been found. The ninth planet in our solar system was Pluto.

The fact that Pluto was discovered at all might be less a case of precise scientific method and more an example of pure dumb luck. It turns out that Percival Lowell's calculations—the ones he used to predict where Planet X should be found—were wrong. Pluto, it has been determined, is too small and too gravitationally weak to influence the orbits of Neptune or Uranus. It would take a much larger object to create a gravitational pull of that magnitude. Therefore, since Lowell's calculations were based on those planets' orbits, they had nothing to do with Pluto. It was just chance that Pluto was within range of the area in which Lowell predicted Planet X should reside. You might say that Clyde Tombaugh, who used Lowell's numbers in his own search for Planet X, was a lucky man.

Two

The Curious Features of Pluto

Pluto may be the smallest and most distant planet in our solar system, but that doesn't mean that scientists are ignoring it. In fact, just the opposite is true. Astronomers realize there is much to learn from Pluto. For that reason they have done everything they can with the technology they have to dissect the planet down to its basic features.

Pluto's Unusual Orbit

Pluto's orbit is extremely unusual. In fact, no other planet in the solar system has an orbit like Pluto's. For one, Pluto's orbit is very long and stretched out (elliptical), like an oval. Pluto's orbit is also positioned at a different angle than the orbits of the other planets. Imagine the other eight planets traveling around the Sun on the same flat plane, one behind the other in eight neat layers as if they were aligned on a table. Then picture Pluto, a tiny planet farther away than all the others, swinging around the Sun at a slightly different angle so that it cuts through the plane (or through the table).

Pluto's strange orbit causes serious problems when it comes to putting the nine planets in order. In fact, while Neptune is widely considered to be the eighth most distant planet from the Sun, located between Uranus, which is number seven, and Pluto, which is number nine, thanks to Pluto's orbit this isn't always the case. Every once in a while—every 228 years, to be exact—Pluto's path dips inside that of Neptune. It then remains closer to the Sun than Neptune for twenty years. When that happens, as it did from 1979 until 1999, Neptune becomes the ninth planet from the Sun and Pluto takes the eighth spot. The next time Pluto will lose its status as the ninth planet in the solar system will be on April 5, 2231.

Pluto by the Numbers

Check out the following facts, compiled by the National Space Science Data Center (NSSDC) and other space-related organizations:

- Mass: 27,600,000,000,000,000,000,000,000 pounds (12,500,000,000,000,000,000,000,000 kilograms). That's just 0.002 times the mass of Earth.
- Volume: 0.0066 times the volume of Earth.
- Diameter: 1,484 miles (2,388 km), making the planet smaller than Earth's Moon and just 0.18 times the diameter of Earth.
- Force of gravity on surface: 0.059 times the gravitational force felt on Earth.
- Satellites: one.
- Day: 153.28 hours (equal to 6.38 days on Earth).
- Average surface temperature: -369° Fahrenheit (-223° Celsius).
- Average distance from the Sun: 3,670,000,000 miles (5,900,000,000 km).
- Year: 248 Earth years.
- Average orbital velocity: 3 miles per second (4.8 km per second)

This artist's rendition of the solar system shows the planets' respective orbits. At the top right is the Sun, which is immediately surrounded by Mercury, Venus, Earth, and Mars. After Mars lies the asteroid belt. Following the asteroid belt are Jupiter, Saturn, Uranus, Neptune, and Pluto. Occasionally, the paths of Neptune and Pluto interchange, temporarily making Neptune the ninth planet from the Sun.

Another interesting fact about Pluto's orbit has to do with the way the planet rotates, or spins on its axis. The speed at which a planet spins on its axis determines the length of its day, while the direction of that spin determines where the Sun will rise and where it will set. Earth, for example, takes twenty-four hours to complete one rotation, so one day on Earth is twenty-four hours long. Also on Earth, the Sun rises in the east and sets in the west. On Pluto, one day lasts more than six Earth days. And Pluto spins in the opposite direction of Earth. This means that on Pluto the Sun rises in the west and sets in the east.

Because Pluto is so far from the Sun and because its path is so elliptical, it has a long way to travel in the course of one orbit. In fact, despite the impressive speed with which Pluto travels through space—scientists have calculated the planet's speed at 10,597 miles per hour (17,054 km/h)—it takes the planet 248 Earth years to orbit the Sun. This means that since its discovery on February 18, 1930, Pluto still has not completed one orbit. You'll have to wait until August 8, 2178, for that.

Pluto's Oddly Shaped Lump

On June 22, 1978, a man named Jim Christy at the United States Naval Observatory in Washington, D.C., discovered something strange. He was studying Pluto's orbit and was working to fine-tune the mathematical calculations scientists use to predict exactly where the planet is in space at any particular time. Christy looked closely at photographs of Pluto as he worked and saw what appeared to be an oddly shaped lump attached to Pluto. It was almost as if the lump were riding piggyback on Pluto's surface.

This is the real-life image of the artist's rendition on page 11. Shown here are Pluto (*left*) and its moon, Charon (*right*). As evidence of just how far these objects are, this is one of the clearest photos available of the planet and the moon. It was taken by the Hubble, the most powerful telescope ever created.

He looked more closely and studied other photographs. He soon realized that the lump was not stationary but was moving around Pluto in a regular pattern. It could only be a moon. Christy named the moon Charon after the Greek and Roman mythological figure who carries the souls of those who die across the river Styx to the underworld.

As far as astronomers can tell, Charon is the only object in space that orbits Pluto. Charon zips around Pluto nearly 12,200 miles (19,630 km) away from the planet. With a diameter of about 700 miles (1,127 km) and a mass of 1,900,000,000,000,000,000,000 kilograms, Charon is the largest moon in the solar system relative to the size of the planet it orbits. It's so big compared to Pluto, in fact, that some scientists have called Pluto and Charon a double planet, feeling that both bodies should be categorized as planets.

Further studies soon showed that Charon's surface is vastly different from Pluto's. Pluto's surface is enveloped in layers of nitrogen and methane ice. Charon's is covered with ice formed from water, like the ice we find here on Earth. What significance does that hold for scientists? Only further investigation will tell.

Three

A Cold, Dark Environment

Were you to land your space capsule on Pluto's surface and take a step outside, what you would see would be completely different from anything you've ever seen before. Pluto is nothing like Earth. There is no water on Pluto—no oceans, lakes, rivers, or streams. No trees or plants exist there either. There is no life on Pluto, at least none that scientists have been able to identify.

All the information scientists have about Pluto's landscape comes from images taken by the Hubble Space Telescope. No spacecraft has ever visited Pluto (although one, called *New Horizons*, is scheduled to in the near future). So everything we know about Pluto has had to be gathered from the analysis of photographs taken of the planet.

The first images of Pluto taken by Hubble were transmitted back to Earth in the mid-1990s. The pictures showed that Pluto had a barren landscape of mountains and valleys. Scientists could tell that these features existed by looking at the contrasts between light and dark. They could see shadows cast by large features on the landscape and brighter areas where the surface was flat compared to the rest of the landscape. Images from Hubble were used to create a map of Pluto's major features. The map was similar to topographical maps (maps that show elevation) that people use on Earth.

How Dark and Cold Is Pluto?

No direct measurements of Pluto's surface temperatures have been taken, but scientists have been able to estimate these temperatures from the images taken by Hubble. Pluto is a dark, cold planet. Almost no sunlight reaches the surface, as Pluto is almost forty times as far from the Sun as Earth is. Imagine staring up into the night sky at a bright star. The amount of light cast from that star would be similar to the amount of light reaching Pluto from the Sun.

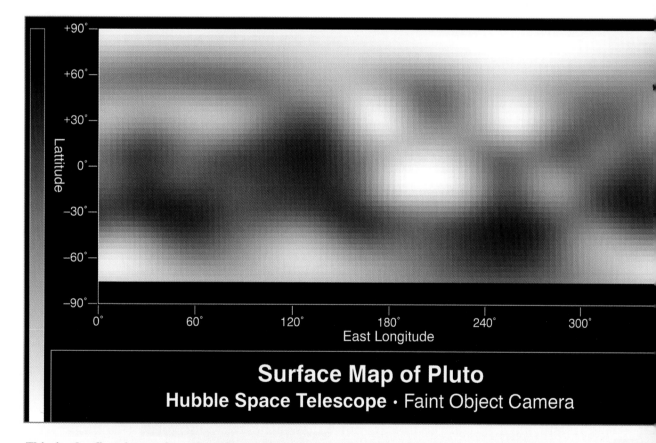

Surface Map of Pluto
Hubble Space Telescope · Faint Object Camera

This is the first image-based surface map ever made of Pluto. The image was taken by the Hubble Space Telescope. The map covers about 85 percent of the planet's surface. The image confirms that Pluto has a dark equator and bright polar caps. The variation in color suggests different landscapes on the planet, such as basins and craters, as well as a varying composition of the surface, including frozen and unfrozen areas.

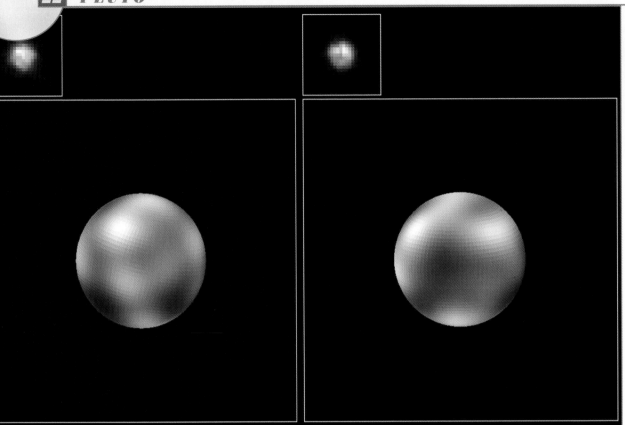

These images of Pluto were taken by the Hubble Space Telescope and show opposite sides (hemispheres) of the planet. Showing how far the planet is and the level of sophistication of Hubble, the larger versions at the bottom are simply enhanced versions of the actual photographs shown in the top left-hand corners.

That lack of sunlight means warmth is hard to come by on Pluto. Scientists have estimated Pluto's surface temperature to be about -369°F (-223°C). That's so cold that almost everything is completely frozen. The only things that don't freeze are certain gases such as neon, hydrogen, and helium.

Because we have yet to visit Pluto and analyze the surface in detail, it is impossible to know for sure what the planet is made of. But because scientists have calculated Pluto's size and mass, they have also been able to determine its density (density is an indication of just how much material is compacted into a certain amount

The Gravity on Pluto

Gravity is the force that keeps us on the ground and prevents us from floating away. You may have seen photographs or videos of astronauts in space, where gravity is so slight that floating is the norm. On Pluto gravity is also minimal, but it is greater than it is in open space.

Gravity is a measure of the attractive forces between two bodies, and it varies according to how big those bodies are. So the reason we don't float off Earth's surface is because Earth is so massive. We are literally pulled toward Earth's center.

Scientists have calculated the gravitational force on Pluto's surface to be just a fraction of that which we experience on Earth. This is because Pluto is so small and so much less massive than Earth. In fact, gravity is so slight that a person on Pluto would weigh just one-fifteenth of what he or she weighs on Earth. You wouldn't float away, but if you jumped as high as you could, you might think you could fly.

of space). By knowing the density of Pluto, scientists can take a guess as to what the planet is made of.

They believe Pluto is made of about 70 percent rock and 30 percent ice. They also think that particularly bright regions in the photographs taken by Hubble indicate the presence of nitrogen ice and solid forms of methane, ethane, and carbon monoxide. The ice is so bright because it reflects light. The scientists are less certain about darker areas of the planet.

Four

Pluto's Elusive Atmosphere

Pluto's climate and weather are mostly mysteries to astronomers at this point. It will be years before they can even begin to know the details of the planet's weather systems and climate trends to the extent that they understand those on Earth. But scientists do know a few things from information they have gleaned from images taken by telescopes both from land and from space. They know, for instance, that Pluto has seasons. The seasons are nothing like those on Earth, but they are distinct.

To understand Pluto's atmosphere, it might help first to take a look at Earth's atmosphere. But let's make something perfectly clear: Without a space suit, you wouldn't last one second on Pluto. The atmosphere at Pluto's surface is far too thin and far too different from that on Earth for humans to survive in.

Earth's atmosphere consists of about 78 percent nitrogen gas and 21 percent oxygen gas. Other gases also exist here, especially carbon dioxide, but they're found in only extremely small amounts. It's this unique blend of invisible gases that allows humans and all forms of life to breathe and grow on Earth.

Pluto's atmosphere, on the other hand, lacks oxygen. Without oxygen, life—at least, life as we know it—cannot exist. Because scientists have never had the chance to take a look at Pluto's atmosphere up close, they know very little about the planet's atmosphere. But they have been able to make some educated guesses.

This is a diagram of what scientists believe is the internal structure of Pluto. Shown in gray is a dense, rocky core that scientists speculate exists within Pluto's center. The outer layer, in blue, is likely composed of ice formed from both water and other substances. To illustrate their relative sizes, the illustration in the lower right-hand corner shows Earth, Pluto, and Charon, from largest to smallest respectively.

How Researchers Study Planets

You might be wondering how astronomers can use telescopes to calculate things like the temperature on Pluto's surface or the composition of the planet's atmosphere. They do so by studying occultations.

Occultations occur when an object far out in space, such as a planet, passes in front of another object that gives off light, such as a star. As the planet (and the atmosphere that surrounds it) crosses the light given off by the star, it causes that light to dim. It's a lot like the solar eclipses we witness from Earth. When the Moon passes in front of the Sun, as occurs from time to time, it temporarily blocks a portion of the Sun's light from view.

Astronomers use their telescopes to make extremely detailed observations of how the starlight changes during an occultation. Once they've recorded these changes and they've seen just how much the light dims as the planet and its atmosphere pass by, they can then turn to their computers to make precise calculations. By observing exactly how much light Pluto's atmosphere filters out, for example, they can determine its density, pressure, and temperature. If they know these things, they can also figure out the composition of the atmosphere.

By studying more than one occultation, scientists can learn about atmospheric changes occurring over time. For example, for the July 2003 issue of the scientific journal *Nature*, a research team studied one occultation in the late 1980s and then another in 2002.

The first occultation these researchers studied occurred in July 1988. They used this occultation to make their initial calculations and determine Pluto's atmospheric composition and temperature. The researchers then used information collected from a 2002 occultation—one that occurred when Pluto passed before a star known as P131.1—to learn about the atmospheric changes that took place since the first occultation.

The latest hope for astronomers using occultations to study planets is a giant plane with a high-tech telescope called the Stratospheric

Observatory for Infrared Astronomy (SOFIA). Scientists at the National Aeronautics and Space Administration (NASA) along with scientists in Germany plan to fly SOFIA around the world to the best places for observing occultations. This will make it much easier for astronomers to watch occultations than it is with their landlocked telescopes. SOFIA should be up and running in 2005.

SOFIA is shown here being prepared for launch to study occultations. All the major components of the telescope were installed. Since the study of occultations requires extreme precision, the instruments aboard SOFIA have to be perfect. Because of this, the engineers working on the telescope go to great lengths to make sure all the vital components are protected. Under SOFIA's red cover to the left is an 8.9-foot (2.7 m) primary mirror. Beneath the aluminum cover to the right is a section of the actual telescope. The plastic wrap around the frame serves as additional protection.

Scientists believe that Pluto's atmosphere is made primarily of the gases nitrogen and methane, as well as a small amount of carbon dioxide. These gases are frozen on Pluto's surface, but they are released in their gaseous forms as Pluto's orbit brings it closer to the Sun. The Sun, providing very little warmth, heats Pluto's surface just enough to thaw the surface out. As the surface thaws, the gases rise and form the atmosphere.

Pluto's atmosphere is extremely thin. In other words, there is not a lot of gas there to make up an atmosphere. Scientists believe this is because the planet is too far away from the Sun for its surface ice to thaw. As Pluto's orbit brings it closer to the Sun, the atmosphere increases slightly. But as the orbit takes it farther away from the Sun, the atmosphere becomes almost nonexistent.

Atmospheric Expansion on Pluto

Now here's the kicker. That last sentence—the one about how the farther Pluto gets from the Sun, the thinner its atmosphere becomes—isn't quite the whole truth. According to a team of astronomers from the Massachusetts Institute of Technology, Boston University, Williams College, Pomona College, Lowell Observatory, and Cornell University, there's a little more to it.

As mentioned previously, for the July 2003 issue of *Nature*, the researchers published a report on observations they took in 2002 while using eight different high-powered telescopes to watch Pluto pass in front of a distant star. By observing how the star grew dimmer as Pluto blocked its light from view, the team was able to calculate certain details about the planet's atmosphere.

What the scientists expected and what they found were two completely different things. The astronomers thought they would

We don't necessarily need sophisticated telescopes to observe occultations. From this perspective on Earth with the naked eye, we can see the crescent moon about to pass in front of Venus, the small, bright body just above it. This image was taken on April 1, 1993, at Mauna Kea, Hawaii.

see that Pluto's atmosphere was cooling as it moved away from the Sun (for the same reasons explained above). They figured the atmosphere would, as a result of this cooling, also be collapsing, or growing thinner. Instead, they found exactly the opposite: Pluto's atmosphere has increased in temperature by about 1.8°F (1°C) since 1989, when the planet was closest to the Sun.

So how could this be? How could the temperature be increasing as Pluto leaves the Sun behind? The researchers think they know. To explain the apparent discrepancy, the astronomers suggested taking a look at the way things work here on Earth. Imagine being outside on a blazing hot day in the middle of summer. In the morning, when the Sun first comes up, things are relatively cool. This makes sense because, keeping in mind how Earth is rotating, this is the point when the Sun is farthest away. Then, as the morning continues and it gets closer to noon, things start to warm up. At exactly noon, the Sun is at its highest point and is as close as it will get the entire day. But here's the catch: It's still getting hotter. The hottest part of the day is not at noon but around 3:00 PM.

Scientists call this the lag effect. The Sun is at its most intense at noon, but it takes a few hours after the most intense point for the temperatures to hit their maximum because it takes time for Earth to heat up. The same thing apparently happens on Pluto, and if you draw a comparison between Pluto's orbit and the time of day here on Earth, it's easy to see why Pluto is getting warmer. If you compare one Pluto year with one Earth day, today, fifteen years after Pluto was closest to the Sun, is equivalent to about 1:15 PM in terms of the lag effect. In other words, it will be another ten years or so before Pluto's lag effect is complete and the planet begins to cool and its atmosphere begins to thin.

Five

The Present and the Future

Many questions about Pluto have already been answered, but many more have yet to be answered. Scientists are interested in this most distant planet from the Sun for many reasons, so you can bet that Pluto will remain a top research priority for years to come.

New Horizons

Currently the best hope we have for learning more about Pluto is in the hands of NASA: a spacecraft called *New Horizons*. *New Horizons* is scheduled for launch on January 9, 2006. From there it will travel to Jupiter. It will then loop around Jupiter in order to get what scientists like to call a gravity boost. That is, it will use Jupiter's gravitational pull to help propel it toward Pluto. Finally, as it continues, *New Horizons* will become the first spaceship to visit Pluto.

The goal of the mission is to fly by both Pluto and its moon, Charon. As it flies by, it will take photographs and collect data. Computers on board the craft will then send the images and information back down to Earth for scientists to analyze. The main goal for NASA scientists is to learn about Pluto's geologic and atmospheric characteristics. They also hope to create detailed maps of the planet's surface. A secondary goal is to learn about Charon's atmosphere and to hunt for other satellites and celestial objects near Pluto.

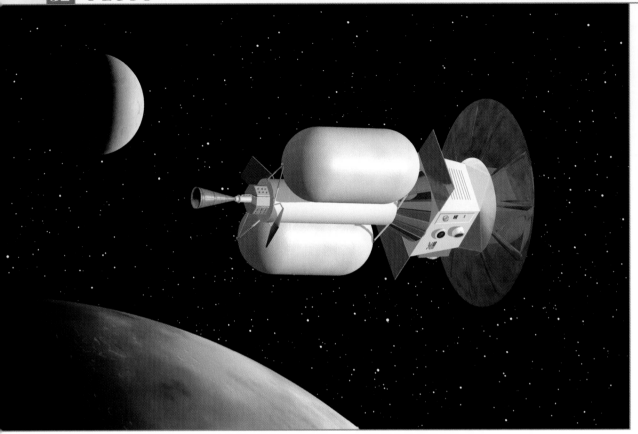

Shown here is an artist's illustration of the *Pluto Kuiper Express*, a probe to Pluto and Charon that has been cancelled for budgetary reasons. To the lower left is Pluto, with Charon in the upper left-hand corner. Before cancellation, the *Pluto Kuiper Express* was scheduled to study Pluto and Charon in a flyby in 2012 and continue on to the Kuiper Belt. Images from the spacecraft would have returned the first close-up images of the bodies and the belt. Many of the responsibilities of the *Pluto Kuiper Express* have been given to the *New Horizons* mission.

The launch will take place in the winter of 2006, but it will take years for *New Horizons* to reach its destination. Astronomers predict the craft will arrive at Pluto in July 2015, traveling on the *Atlas V* rocket.

Six months before it flies by Pluto, *New Horizons* will be in close enough range for its computers to begin collecting data on the planet. By gathering information so early in the mission, *New Horizons* will be able to study both of Pluto's hemispheres instead of just the one that will face the spacecraft at closest approach. *New Horizons* will not be able to fly around Pluto. The craft will make one rather quick pass by the planet and then continue deeper into space.

So how close will *New Horizons* come to Pluto? It will fly within 5,960 miles (9,600 km) of the planet at a speed of 7 miles per second (11 km/s). Its images of Charon will be from almost three times that distance, 16,000 miles (26,000 km). It may seem like 5,960 miles is very far away, but it's close enough to allow *New Horizons* to take pictures so detailed that scientists back on Earth will be able to see and map every little dip and rise on Pluto's surface.

Traveling at 7 miles per second (11 km/s), it won't be long before *New Horizons* leaves Pluto behind. When it does, however, its mission will not be over. After Pluto, the spacecraft will continue through the Kuiper Belt. In addition to Pluto, the Kuiper Belt contains numerous small, icy, cometlike objects. *New Horizons* will transmit images and other data gathered from these objects back to Earth for up to ten years after it passes Pluto.

The Great Debate: Is Pluto Really a Planet?

For years there have been astronomers who have argued that Pluto should not even be classified as a planet. Their reasons are simple. For one, they believe that Pluto might have been formed by a different process from the one that formed the other planets, perhaps as a result of a massive collision between objects in space. They also think that Pluto was likely guided into its current orbit by the gravitational forces of Neptune. Finally, they say

A High-Tech Endeavor

The *New Horizons* spacecraft, as you might expect, is extremely high-tech. Triangular in shape, it includes an 8-foot-wide (2.4 m wide) radio dish fastened to one side. The dish will be used for communications between the craft and scientists on Earth. *New Horizons* will also be fitted with multiple "star cameras" for use in steering and navigation. Finally, it will contain several important scientific instruments, including the Long Range Reconnaissance Imager (LORRI), the Pluto Exploration Remote Sensing Investigation (PERSI), the Radio Science Experiment (REX), and two charged-particle detectors.

These instruments may sound complicated, and they are. But they're not so hard to understand that nonscientists can't get an idea of what they do. LORRI, built by a physics laboratory at Johns Hopkins University in Maryland, will be used to create high-resolution maps of Pluto from long distances. PERSI includes three special sensors designed to collect data from visible, infrared, and ultraviolet light. REX will be used to gather information about Pluto's atmosphere and surface temperature. The charged-particle detectors will take a look at the tiny particles (ions and electrons) that manage to escape Pluto's atmosphere.

New Horizons and its various instruments are being built in different parts of the country, where everything will be ready for final assembly. It will be up to engineers to ensure that all systems are go for the 2006 launch.

that Pluto, at a mere 1,484 miles (2,388 km) in diameter, is not big enough to be a planet. In fact, they say, it's not even as big as some of the moons (including Earth's) found in our solar system. If it's not as big as a moon, they argue, why should it be given planetary status? It could be a comet, maybe, or perhaps an asteroid, but not a planet.

Shown here is an artist's illustration of *New Horizons*. The object to the right is one of the millions of icy bodies in the Kuiper Belt, just beyond the orbit of Neptune. *New Horizons* is scheduled to study the Kuiper Belt as well as Pluto and Charon. An extremely high-tech spacecraft, it has an 8-foot-wide (2.4 m wide) radio dish, which will relay messages back to scientists on Earth. This is in addition to many other technical devices designed to study one of the most remote and mysterious planets.

Today, although dissenters still exist, most astronomers agree that Pluto is in fact the ninth planet (eighth when it switches orbit with Neptune) in the solar system. The debate will likely continue for many years, as those on both sides have good points. The main issue at stake, however, seems to be how to define a planet. Does a planet have to be a certain size? Does it have to follow a particular orbit? How small can it be relative to its moon or moons? The answers to these questions remain to be seen.

The debate has also been fueled by the discovery of Quaoar and Sedna, two of the largest bodies spotted orbiting the Sun since the discovery of Pluto. Both of these bodies are smaller than Pluto. Quaoar is about 40 percent of Pluto's size. Sedna's accurate size is still being determined, although it is probably larger than Quaoar. The discovery of these objects is raising the question among scientists of how a planet should be defined.

What's Next for Pluto?

Pluto will continue, as it has for billions of years, to orbit the Sun as one of the nine planets in our solar system. And as it does, scientists will continue to train their telescopes to the sky and study every last detail of its motion. Using data they collect on Pluto and other planets, they'll learn more about how objects in space influence each other. They'll probably try to determine Pluto's ultimate fate: Will it burn out one day when it comes too close to the Sun? Will it collide with another massive object in space and explode into trillions of pieces? Will it change shape or speed or size? Or will it just continue on its same path forever?

NASA is working to solve many of the mysteries of space, and Pluto is just one of them. Each year, progress is made with each new

Shown here is an artist's illustration of the planetoid Quaoar. Until November 2003, when the body Sedna was first spotted, Quaoar was the largest object to be discovered orbiting the Sun since the discovery of Pluto in 1930. After some debate, scientists now consider Quaoar too small to be classified as a planet—it is about 40 percent the size of Pluto. The discoveries of both Quaoar and Sedna are making scientists wonder whether a specific definition for a planet is needed.

launch of a space shuttle weighed down with high-tech experiments and with each new million-dollar telescope designed to look just a bit deeper into space.

Much of what we now know about Pluto has been taken from the data collected by just a few telescopes. In the future there will be far more data collected from the *New Horizons* mission. Someday, if technology allows it, a mission to Pluto will include an astronaut on board. And maybe, if you're up to the challenge, that astronaut will be you.

1908: Percival Lowell writes about what he believes is another planet that is located somewhere beyond Neptune. He believes that Planet X, as he calls it, exists because the orbits of Neptune and Uranus seem to be influenced by the gravity of another celestial object.

William Henry Pickering of the Harvard College Observatory in Massachusetts publishes a report justifying his belief in the existence of what he calls Planet O. Pickering also predicts the existence of several other planets in addition to Planet O. He names them Planets P, Q, R, and S.

1927: Researchers at the Lowell Observatory in Arizona decide to renew the search for Pluto by using their new state-of-the-art telescope.

1930: After looking at one of the many photographs taken with the Lowell telescope, Clyde Tombaugh finds a faint object that has never been charted on any map. Tombaugh and his colleagues withhold their discovery for almost a month while they work to ensure that the object in the photograph is in fact the missing planet.

2006: The *New Horizons* spacecraft is scheduled for launch on January 9, 2006. It will travel first to Jupiter, which will give it a gravity boost to propel it to Pluto. The goal of the mission is to learn about Pluto's geologic and atmospheric characteristics. Scientists also hope to create detailed maps of Pluto's surface. Secondary goals are to learn about the atmosphere of Pluto's moon, Charon, and to hunt for other satellites and celestial objects near Pluto.

2015: Astronomers predict that the *New Horizons* spacecraft will arrive at Pluto in July.

Glossary

astronaut A person trained to travel to space in a spacecraft.

astronomer A scientist who studies space.

atmosphere The mixture of gases that surrounds a planet.

axis An imaginary line through the center of an object around which that object rotates.

colonize To move to a place and establish a settlement there.

data Information collected as part of a scientific study.

density A measurement of the amount of material contained in a specific area of space.

diameter The length of a straight line through the center of an object.

ellipse A shape resembling an oval or elongated circle.

gravity A force that attracts anything that has mass.

hemisphere One half of a sphere.

Kuiper Belt A ring of small, often icy objects in the solar system just beyond the orbit of Neptune.

lag effect The delay in the rise in temperature of a planet after the Sun has passed its period of most intense light.

mass The amount of material contained within an object.

observatory A building that houses a telescope and other instruments used for observing and studying space.

occultation An interruption of light caused when a celestial body passes in front of another.

orbit The path a planet or other object in space takes as it revolves around something else.

satellite A relatively small object that orbits another larger object.

solar system The Sun and the celestial bodies that revolve around it.

spacecraft A vehicle designed to explore space and objects in space.

telescope An instrument designed to magnify far-off objects for study.

topography The vertical dimensions of a landscape, including hills, mountains, and valleys.

velocity The speed of an object in a certain direction or trajectory.

volume The amount of space an object contains.

For More Information

Goddard Space Flight Center
Code 130
Office of Public Affairs
Greenbelt, MD 20771
(301) 286-8955
e-mail: gsfcpao@pop100.gsfc.nasa.gov
Web site: http://www.gsfc.nasa.gov

Jet Propulsion Laboratory
4800 Oak Grove Drive
Pasadena, CA 91109
(818) 354-4321
Web site: http://www.jpl.nasa.gov

Museum of Science
Science Park
Boston, MA 02114
(617) 723-2500
Web site: http://www.mos.org

National Aeronautics and Space Administration (NASA)
Headquarters Information Center
Washington, DC 20546-0001
(202) 358-0000
Web site: http://www.nasa.gov

Smithsonian National Air and Space Museum
6th and Independence Avenue SW
Washington, DC 20560
(202) 357-2700
Web site: http://www.nasm.si.edu

Space Telescope Science Institute (STSCI)
3700 San Martin Drive
Baltimore, MD 21218
(410) 338-4444
Web site: http://www.stsci.edu

Web Sites

Due to the changing nature of Internet links, the Rosen Publishing Group, Inc., has developed an online list of Web sites related to the subject of this book. This site is updated regularly. Please use this link to access the list:

http://www.rosenlinks.com/lnp/plut

For Further Reading

Davies, John. *Beyond Pluto: Exploring the Outer Limits of the Solar System.* Cambridge, UK: Cambridge University Press, 2001.

Goss, Tim. *Uranus, Neptune, and Pluto* (The Universe). Oxford, England: Heinemann Library, 2003.

Littmann, Mark. *Planets Beyond: Discovering the Outer Solar System.* New York: John Wiley & Sons, Inc., 1988.

Stern, Alan, and Jacqueline Mitton. *Pluto and Charon: Ice Worlds on the Ragged Edge of the Solar System.* New York: John Wiley & Sons, Inc., 1997.

Tocci, Salvatore. *A Look at Pluto.* New York: Franklin Watts, Inc., 2003.

Vogt, Gregory L. *Pluto* (The Gateway Solar System). Brookfield, CT: Millbrook Press, 1996.

Bibliography

NASA National Space Science Data Center Web Site. "Pluto." Retrieved August 5, 2003 (http://nssdc.gsfc.nasa.gov/planetary/planets/plutopage.html).

NASA Solar System Exploration Web Site. "Neptune." Retrieved August 8, 2003 (http://solarsystem.nasa.gov/features/planets/neptune/neptune.html).

The Nine Planets Web Site. "A Multimedia Tour of the Solar System." Retrieved August 23, 2003 (http://www.nineplanets.org).

Smithsonian National Air and Space Museum Web Site. Retrieved August 15, 2003 (http://www.nasm.si.edu).

Solar Views Web Site. "Neptune." Retrieved August 22, 2003 (http://www.solarviews.com/eng/neptune.htm).

Index

About the Author

Chris Hayhurst is a writer living in Colorado.

Photo Credits

Cover, p. 16 © David A. Hardy/Science Photo Library/Photo Researchers, Inc.; pp. 4–5 © NASA/Science Photo Library/Photo Researchers, Inc.; p. 8 © Tony and Daphne Hallas/Science Photo Library/Photo Researchers, Inc.; pp. 9, 12, 32 © Science Photo Library/Photo Researchers, Inc.; p. 11 © Detlev Van Ravenswaay/Science Photo Library/Photo Researchers, Inc.; pp. 18, 22 NASA/NSSDC; p. 21 NASA/Alan Stern (Southwest Research Institute)/Marc Buie (Lowell Observatory)/NASA and ESA; p. 25 © Mark Garlick/Science Photo Library/Photo Researchers, Inc.; p. 27 NASA/USRA; p. 29 © McGrath Photography/Science Photo Library/Photo Researchers, Inc.; p. 35 NASA/Southwest Research Institute/Johns Hopkins University Applied Physics Laboratory; p. 37 NASA and M. Brown (CalTech).

Designer: Thomas Forget; Editor: Nicholas Croce